A Special Gift

For

_____

From

_____

Date

_____

Message

_____

_____

Flowers

of

Love

~ Helen Steiner Rice ~

Fleming H. Revell
A Division of Baker Book House Co
Grand Rapids, Michigan 49516

Wings Of Love

The priceless gift of life is love,
for with the help of God above,
love can change the human race
and make this world a better place.
For love dissolves all hate and fear
and makes our vision bright and clear
So we can see and rise above
our pettiness on wings of love.

I Love You

I love you for so many things,
I don't know where to start,
But most of all I love you
for your understanding heart —
A heart that makes you thoughtful
and considerate and kind,
A heavenly combination
that is difficult to find.
And I can't help the feeling
that loving folks like you
Sent out so many thought waves
that my dearest dream came true.

The Key

Love is a gift
to treasure forever
Given by God
without price tag or measure ...
Love is a gift
we can all possess,
Love is a key
to the soul's happiness!

What Is Love?

What is love?
>no words can define it –
It's something so great
>only God could design it.
Wonder of wonders,
>beyond man's conception,
And only in God
>can love find true perfection.
For love means much more
>than small words can express,
For what man calls love
>is so very much less
Than the beauty and depth
>and the true richness of
God's gift to mankind –
>His compassionate love.
For love has become
>a word that's misused,
Perverted, distorted,
>and often abused

speak of light romance
    or some affinity for
passing attraction
    that is seldom much more
an a mere interlude
    or inflamed fascination,
romantic fling
    of no lasting duration.
t love is enduring
    and patient and kind,
judges all things
    with the heart, not the mind.
r love is unselfish –
    giving more than it takes –
d no matter what happens,
    love never forsakes.
s faithful and trusting
    and always believing,
uileless and honest
    and never deceiving.
s, love is beyond
    what man can define,
r love is immortal
    and God's gift is divine.

Love Works In Wondrous Ways

With love in our hearts,
let us try this year
To lift the clouds
of hate and fear,
For love works in ways
that are wondrous and strange,
And there is nothing in life
that love cannot change.

The True Gift

With our hands we give gifts
    that money can buy –
diamonds that sparkle
    like stars in the sky,
trinkets that glitter
    like the sun as it rises,
beautiful baubles
    that come as surprises –
but only our hearts
    can feel real love
and share the gift
    of our Father above.

The Magic Of Love

Love is like magic
        and it always will be,
For love still remains
        life's sweet mystery.
Love works in ways
        that are wondrous and strange,
And there's nothing in life
        that love cannot change.
Love can transform
        the most commonplace
Into beauty and splendor
        and sweetness and grace.
Love is unselfish,
        understanding, and kind,

For it sees with its heart
and not with its mind.
Love is the answer
that everyone seeks.
Love is the language
that every heart speaks.
Love can't be bought –
it's priceless and free.
Love, like pure magic,
is a sweet mystery.

A Prayer For Those We Love

Our Father, who art in heaven,
hear this little prayer
And reach across the miles today
that stretch from here to there,
So I may feel much closer
to those I'm fondest of,
And they may know I think of them
with thankfulness and love.
And help all people everywhere
who must often dwell apart
To know that they're together
in the haven of the heart.

A Priceless Treasure

Love is like a priceless treasure
which there is no way to measure.
For who can fathom stars or sea
or figure the length of eternity?
Love's too great to understand,
but just to clasp a loved one's hand
Can change the darkness into light
and make the heart take wingless flight,
And blessed are they who walk in love,
for love's a gift from God above.

Everyone Needs Someone

People need people,
and friends need friends,
And we all need love,
for a full life depends
Not on vast riches
or great acclaim,
Not on success
or worldly fame,
But just on knowing
that someone cares
And holds us close
in thoughts and prayers.
For only the knowledge
that we're understood
Makes everyday living
feel wonderfully good.

d we rob ourselves
ife's greatest need
nen we lock up our hearts
d fail to heed
e outstretched hand
ching to find
kindred spirit
ose heart and mind
e lonely and longing
omehow share
r joys and sorrows
d to make us aware
at life's completeness
d richness depend
the things we share
h our loved ones and friends.

Love's Test

Dear God,
Please help me in my feeble way
To somehow do something each day
To show the one I love the best
My faith in him will stand each test.
And let me show in some small way
The love I have for him each day
And prove beyond all doubt and fear
That his love for me I hold most dear.
And so I ask of God above –
Just make me worthy of his love.

Deep In My Heart

Happy little memories
        go flitting through my mind,
And in all my thoughts and memories
        I always seem to find
The picture of your face, dear,
        the memory of your touch,
And all the other little things
        I've come to love so much.
You cannot go beyond my thoughts
        or leave my love behind,
Because I keep you in my heart
        and forever in my mind.
And though I may not tell you,
        I think you know it's true
That I find daily happiness
        in the very thought of you.

If I Had Loved You Then

If I had known you way back when,
I might have loved you even then,
But, oh, what a difference there would have been
If instead of now, I'd loved you then.
Our love might have burned with a brighter flame,
we'd have toasted our fame in bubbling champagne,
We'd have loved and been lost in a world of fun,
and now our young love would be over and done.
But meeting each other in the gold, autumn haze
has brought deeper meaning to the last, golden days.

The Joys Of Remembering

There's a heap of satisfaction
        to sit here thinking of you
and to tell you once again, dear,
        how very much I love you.
There is comfort just in longing
        for a smile from your dear face
and joy in just remembering
        each sweet and fond embrace.
There is happiness in knowing
        that my heart will always be
a place where I can hold you
        and keep you near to me.

It's such a quiet, lovely thing,
        it doesn't ask for much,
It isn't untamed longing
        that cries for passion's touch,
It's not built upon the quicksand
        of a pair of lips and arms,
For only false foundations
        are raised on physical charms,
I wish that I could tell you
        about this thing I feel,
It's intangible like gossamer,
        but like a hoop of steel

binds me very close to you
and opens up the door
more real, deep contentment
than I've ever known before.
you see, your music reaches
beyond where words dare pass.
's like a soul's communion
or a sacred, holy mass.
s something indefinable,
like a sea and sky and sod –
might just be enchantment,
but I like to think it's God.

Happiness

You put the *love* in loveliness
  and the *sweet* in sweetness, too.
I think they took life's dearest things
  and wrapped them up in you.
And when I send good wishes,
  they're filled with love so true,
And I hope the year will bring you
  the joy that is your due.
For when I think of you, dear,
  I can't forget the thought
Of how much real, true happiness
  just knowing you has brought.

Remembrance Road

There's a road I call remembrance
where I walk each day with you.
It's a pleasant, happy road, my dear,
all filled with memories true.
Today it leads me through a spot
where I can dream awhile,
And in its tranquil peacefulness
I touch your hand and smile.
There are hills and fields and budding trees
and stillness that's so sweet
That it seems that this must be the place
where God and humans meet.
I hope we can go back again
and golden hours renew,
And God go with you always, dear,
until the day we do.

My Love For You

There are things we cannot measure,
    like the depths of waves and sea
And the heights of stars in heaven
    and the joy you bring to me.
Like eternity's long endlessness
    and the sunset's golden hue,
There is no way to measure
    the love I have for you.

In Your Heart

Keep me in your heart, dear,
    and in your every prayer,
For wherever you are, darling,
    I like to feel I'm there.

The Magic Of Your Presence

I come to you when day is done
and find you waiting there,
And with your magic fingertips
the heavy robe of care
Slips from my heart
and roses bloom,
Because your presence
fills the room.

What Is Marriage

It is sharing and caring,
giving and forgiving,
loving and being loved,
walking hand in hand,
talking heart to heart,
seeing through each other's eyes,
laughing together,
weeping together,
praying together,
and always trusting and believing
and thanking God for each other.
For love that is shared is a beautiful thing
It enriches the soul and makes the heart sing.

The Joy Of Love

Love is a many-splendored thing,
      the greatest joy that life can bring,
And let no one try to disparage
      the sacred bond of holy marriage,
For love is not love until God above
      sanctifies the union of two people in love.

Lasting Love

Love is much more than a tender caress
and more than bright hours of happiness,
For a lasting love is made up of sharing
both hours that are joyous and also despairing.
It's made up of patience and deep understanding
and never of stubborn or selfish demanding.
It's made up of climbing the steep hills together
and facing with courage life's stormiest weather.
And nothing on earth or in heaven can part
a love that has grown to be part of the heart.
And just like the sun and the stars and the sea,
this love will go on through eternity,
For true love lives on when earthly things die,
for it's part of the spirit that soars to the sky.

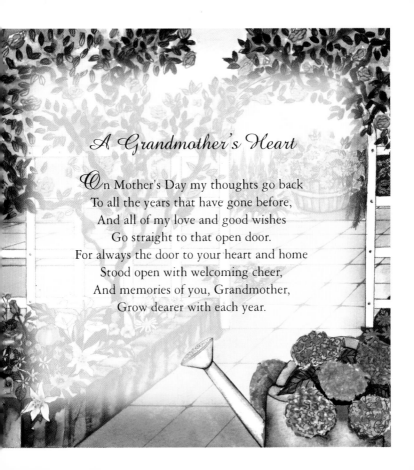

A Grandmother's Heart

On Mother's Day my thoughts go back
To all the years that have gone before,
And all of my love and good wishes
Go straight to that open door.
For always the door to your heart and home
Stood open with welcoming cheer,
And memories of you, Grandmother,
Grow dearer with each year.

Anniversary Thoughts

It takes a special day like this
      to just look back and reminisce
And think of things you used to do
      when love was young and so were you.
But all things change, for that is life,
      and love between a man and wife
Cannot remain romantic bliss
      forever flavored with a kiss.
But always there's the bond of love
      that there is no explaining of,
And through the trials of life it grows
      like flowers do beneath the snows.

Sometimes it's hidden from the sight
just like the sun gives way to night,
But always there's that bond of love
that there is no explaining of.
And every year that you're together,
regardless of the kind of weather,
That bond of love keeps growing stronger
because you've shared it one year longer.
And it's a pleasure I wouldn't miss,
wishing you joy on a day like this,
And may the good Lord up above
look down today and bless your love.

Fathers Are Wonderful People

Fathers are wonderful people,
       too little understood,
And we do not sing their praises
       as often as we should.
For somehow Father seems to be
       the man who pays the bills,
While Mother binds up little hurts
       and nurses all our ills.
And Father struggles daily
       to live up to his image
As protector and provider
       and the hero of the scrimmage.
And perhaps this is the reason
       we sometimes get the notion
That fathers are not subject
       to the thing we call emotion,
But if you look inside Dad's heart,
       where no one else can see,
You'll find he's sentimental
       and as soft as he can be.

but he's so busy every day
          in the gruelling race of life
that he leaves the sentimental stuff
          to his partner and his wife.

But fathers are just wonderful
          in a million different ways
and they merit loving compliments
          and accolades of praise,
for the only reason Dad aspires
          to fortune and success
to make the family proud of him
          and to bring them happiness.
And like our heavenly Father,
          he's a guardian and guide –
someone we can count on
          to be always on our side.

A Mother's Love Is A Haven
In The Storms Of Life

A mother's love is like an island
     in life's ocean vast and wide –
A peaceful, quiet shelter
     from the restless, rising tide.
A mother's love is like a fortress,
     and we seek protection there
When the waves of tribulation
     seem to drown us in despair.
A mother's love is a sanctuary
     where our souls can find sweet rest
From the struggle and the tension
     of life's fast and futile quest.
A mother's love is like a tower
     rising far above the crowd,
And her smile is like the sunshine
     breaking through a threatening cloud.

A mother's love is like a beacon
　　　burning bright with faith and prayer,
And through the changing scenes of life
　　　we can find a haven there.
For a mother's love is fashioned
　　　after God's enduring love –
It is endless and unfailing
　　　like the love of Him above.
For God knew, in His great wisdom,
　　　that He couldn't be everywhere,
So He put His little children
　　　in a loving mother's care.

The Gift Of God's Love

It can't be bought,
      it can't be sold,
It can't be measured
      in silver and gold.
It's a special wish
      that God above
Will fill your heart
      with peace and love –
The love of God,
      which is divine,
That is beyond
      what words can define
So you may know
      the comfort of
God's all-fulfilling
      grace and love.

Somebody Cares

Somebody cares and always will —
the world forgets, but God loves you still.
You cannot go beyond His love
no matter what you're guilty of,
For God forgives until the end —
He is your faithful, loyal friend,
And though you try to hide your face,
there is no shelter any place
That can escape His watchful eye,
for on the earth and in the sky
He's ever-present and always there
to take you in His tender care
And bind the wounds and mend the breaks
when all the world around forsakes.
Somebody cares and loves you still,
and God is the Someone who always will.

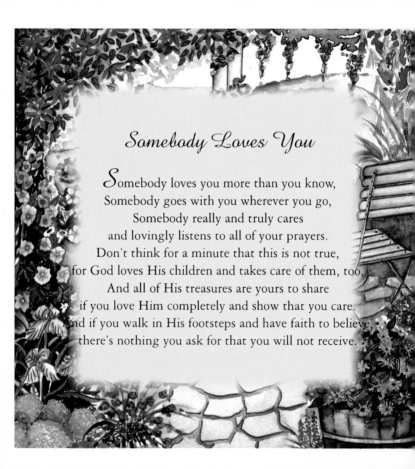

Somebody Loves You

Somebody loves you more than you know,
Somebody goes with you wherever you go,
Somebody really and truly cares
and lovingly listens to all of your prayers.
Don't think for a minute that this is not true,
for God loves His children and takes care of them, too,
And all of His treasures are yours to share
if you love Him completely and show that you care.
And if you walk in His footsteps and have faith to believe,
there's nothing you ask for that you will not receive.

Strangers Are Friends
We Haven't Met

God knows no strangers, He loves us all –
    the poor, the rich, the great, the small.
He is a friend who is always there
    to share our troubles and lessen our care.
For no one is a stranger in God's sight,
    for God is love, and in His light
May we, too, try in our small way
    to make new friends from day to day.
So pass no stranger with an unseeing eye,
    for God may be sending a new friend by.

Grant Us Hope And Faith And Love

Hope for a world grown cynically cold,
hungry for power and greedy for gold,
Faith to believe when, within and without,
there's a nameless fear in a world of doubt.
Love that is bigger than race or creed
to cover the world and fulfill each need ...
God grant these gifts of faith, hope, and love –
three things this world has so little of –
for only these gifts from our Father above
can turn man's sins from hatred to love.

No Favor Do I Seek Today

I come not to ask, to plead, or implore You,
I just come to tell You how much I adore You.
For to kneel in Your presence makes me feel blessed,
for I know that You know all my needs best,
And it fills me with joy just to linger with You,
As my soul You replenish and my heart You renew.
For prayer is much more than just asking for things –
It's the peace and contentment that quietness brings.
So thank You again for Your mercy and love
And for making me heir to Your kingdom above.

Dear God, You Are Love

Dear God, You are a part of me
You're all I hear and all I see,
You're what I say and what I do
For all my life belongs to You.
You walk with me and You talk with me,
For I am Yours eternally.
And when I stumble, slip, and fall
Because I'm weak and lost and small,
You help me up and take my hand
And lead me toward the Promised Land.
I cannot dwell apart from You,
You would not ask or want me to,
For You have room within Your heart
To make each child of Yours a part
Of You, and all your *love* and Care.
For God, You are *love* and
love should be everywhere!

Priceless Gifts

This brings you a million good wishes and more
For the things you cannot buy in a store –
A joy-filled heart and a happy smile,
Faith to sustain you in times of trial,
Contentment, inner peace, and love –
All priceless gifts from God above!

Remember This

Great is the power of might and mind,
but only love can make us kind,
And all we are or hope to be
is empty pride and vanity.
If love is not a part of all,
the greatest man is very small.

Across The Miles

I think of you so many times
and wish with all my heart
That I could reach across the miles
that keep us far apart
And somehow just communicate
the things I'd like to say
If I were standing close to you
instead of far away.

The Love Of God

The love of God
is too great to conceive.
Don't try to explain it —
just trust and believe!

God Is Love

God is love,
and He made the human heart
capable of this great miracle of love
so that we might glimpse heaven
and experience that divine touch.